THE KNIT PARADE

12 statement sweater patterns,
12 motifs to meddle with

THE KNIT
PARADE

Rebecca Rymsza

COLLINS & BROWN

WHERES ME JUMPER?

06   Introduction

THE BASICS

08   Before you start knitting...

THE SWEATER PATTERNS

10   Are 'Friends' Electric?

16   Lucky Star

22   Picture This

28   Me Jane

34   Mr Moustache

40   Paint It Black

46   Spring

52   On Repeat

58   Telephone

64   Bad Girls

70   Weather Experience

76   Envy

THE EXTRAS

82   Applying motifs
        to other items

GO RENEGADE

84   Polka dots

88   Stripes

92   Zig zags

96   Diagonals

100   Checks

104   Hearts

AND FINALLY

108   Knit Parade playlist

109   Wheres Me Jumper

110   Acknowledgements

Jumper, sweater...

...however you say it, that's what we make at Wheres Me Jumper. Our customers send us their designs, images and ideas and we create a bespoke jumper that's totally unique to them.

Now you can have a go at creating a sweater unique to you.

You'll find inside this book a series of patterns as a guide (with a nod to some of our favourite bands and songs), but there are no rules. So pick a colour, any colour, and make what suits you.

There is also a section at the back of the book with basic graphic knitting patterns. Use one or use them all, however you like. You might be a polka-dot prince, or princess, and choose to stick to one pattern (that's polka dots, if we lost you), or you might want to channel the Fresh Prince, circa 1991, in which case, we salute you.

So peruse it, use it and you can totally abuse it.

Have fun!
Love, Beki

Before you start knitting...

MATERIALS

Things you will definitely need
– A pair of 3.25mm (US 3) knitting needles
– A pair of 4mm (US 6) knitting needles
– Two stitch holders
– Tapestry needle

Things you might need
A set of 3.25mm (US 3) circular needles, 40cm (16in) long, for working neckband in the round.

YARN AND TENSION

We've knitted the jumpers in this book using Jarol Heritage DK yarn; (Double Knit weight; 55% wool, 25% acrylic, 20% nylon; 250m/273yds per 100g ball). It's a nice yarn and not too expensive, but you can use any DK yarn that knits to the tension of 22 stitches and 28 rows over 10cm (4in). Just be sure to knit a tension square so you don't end up with your arms at your knees. Embarrassing.

ABBREVIATIONS

alt – alternate
cast off – bind off
cont – continue
dec – decrease by knitting (RS) or purling (WS) two stitches together
inc – increase by knitting into front and back of stitch
k – knit
LH – left hand
p – purl
rem – remain(ing)
rep – repeat
RH – right hand
RS – right side (of work)
st(s) – stitch(es)
St-st – stocking stitch; knit one row, purl one row
WS – wrong side (of work)

SIZING GUIDE

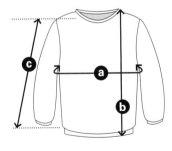

	S–M	M–L
a. Chest	94cm (37in)	108cm (42.5in)
b. Length	58cm (23in)	63cm (25in)
c. Sleeves	51cm (20in)	56cm (22in)

CHANGING COLOURS

If you are working fairisle, carry yarn loosely across the back of your work and never over more than 7 stitches. When working in intarsia, use a separate ball of wool for each section of colour (make your own small balls of wool) and twist yarn at the back of your work so you don't make any holes!

LET'S GET STARTED

Are 'Friends' Electric?

*It's cold outside and the paint's
peeling off of my walls*

Are 'Friends' Electric?

BEFORE YOU START

Materials
– Jarol Heritage DK – Yarn A: 6(7) balls in Silver Grey shade 134; 1 ball each in Yarn B: Black shade 112; Yarn C: Gold shade 140
– A pair of 3.25mm (US 3) knitting needles
– A pair of 4mm (US 6) knitting needles
– A set of 3.25mm (US 3) circular needles, 40cm (16in) long; (optional for working neckband in the round)
– Two stitch holders
– Tapestry needle

Sizes
S/M – To fit chest 86.5–91.5cm (34–36in), actual measurement 94cm (37in)
M/L – To fit chest 96.5–102cm (38–40in), actual measurement 108cm (42.5in)

Tension
22 sts and 28 rows to 10cm (4in) in stocking stitch on 4mm needles. Take time to check your tension and adjust as necessary to ensure an accurate fit.

SWEATER

Back
With 3.25mm needles and yarn A, cast on 98(110) sts.
Row 1 (RS): [K1, p1] rep to end. This row sets rib.
Work a further 14(14) rows in rib.
Next row (WS): Work as set in rib and **at the same time** inc 7(11) sts evenly across the row. 105(121) sts *
Change to 4mm needles and starting with a k row, work in St-st until your work measures approx. 58(63)cm / 23(25)in from cast-on edge ending with a WS row.

Shape shoulders
Next row (RS): Cast off 35(42) sts, k35(37), cast off 35(42) sts and place remaining sts on hold.

Front
Work as for Back to * then cont as follows:
Change to 4mm needles and starting with a k row, work 32(40) rows in St-st or until your work measures approx. 17(20)cm / 6¾(8)in from cast-on edge ending with a WS row.

Commence chart:
Row 1 (RS): With A, k63(71), join B, k1(1), with A, k to end.
Row 2 (WS): With A, p41(49), with B, p2(2), with A, k to end.
Cont as set until row 70 of chart is complete.
Cont with A only and work 20(26) rows in St-st, or until your work measures approx. 49(54)cm / 19(21½)in from cast-on edge, ending with a WS row.

Shape neck
Next row (RS): K43(50), turn your work so WS is facing, dec 1 st, p to end, turn. Cont on these sts, leaving remaining sts on hold.
** Dec 1 st at neck edge every row until 40(47) sts remain, then dec 1 st every other row until 35(42) sts remain.
Work 11(11) rows straight in St-st and cast off. ***
With RS facing, rejoin yarn at neck edge and k19(21), then slip these sts to holder for neckband and k to end of row.
Work as RH side from ** to ***.

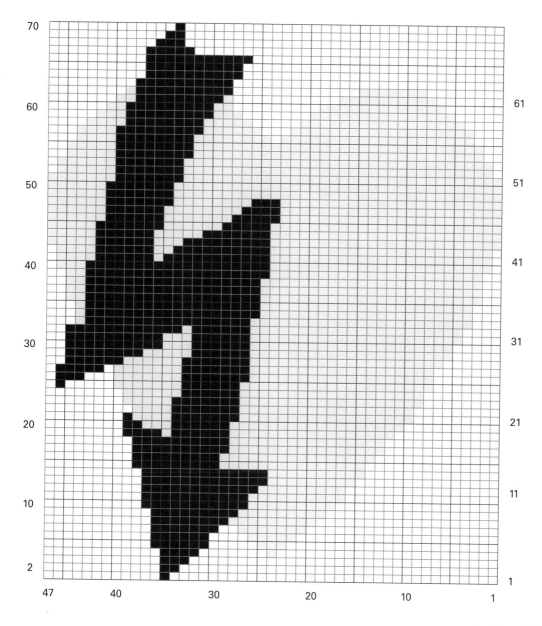

Sleeves (make two)

With 3.25mm needles and yarn A, cast on 48(52) sts.

Row 1 (RS): [K1, p1] rep to end. This row sets rib.

Work a further 14 rows in rib.

Next row (WS): Work as set in rib and **at the same time** inc 7(7) sts evenly across the row. 55(59) sts

Change to 4mm needles and starting with a k row, work in St-st and **at the same time** inc 1 st at each end of every sixth row a total of 11(13) times. 77(85) sts

Cont straight in St-st until your work measures approx. 51(56)cm / 20(22)in from cast-on edge.

Cast off loosely.

Neckband

You can do this in one of two ways depending on your preference:

Using straight needles: Join Front and Back pieces at RH shoulder. Using a 3.25mm needle and A, beginning at LH shoulder with RS facing, pick up and k28(28) sts down LH front, work 19(21) held sts, pick up and k28(28) sts up RH side, work 35(37) held sts. 106(110) sts

Work in k1, p1 rib for 7 rows, knit 1 row, work rib for 7 rows. Cast off loosely in rib.

Using circular needles: Join both shoulder seams. With 3.25mm needle and A, beginning at LH shoulder with RS facing, pick up and k26(26) sts down LH front, work 19(21) held sts, pick up and k26(26) sts up RH side, work 35(37) held sts. 104(108) sts

Join for working in the round placing a marker to indicate beginning of round, work k1, p1 rib for 7 rounds, purl 1 round, work rib for 7 rounds. Cast off loosely in rib.

Making up

If using straight needles join LH shoulder.

Turn garment inside out so WS is facing, fold neckband over and loosely stitch into place on WS and so it does not pull tight.

Lay garment out flat, pin sleeves into position with centre point of cast-off edge lined up to shoulder seam and stitch into place.

Join side and sleeve seams.

Gently block to measurements shown on page 8.

Lucky Star

You shine on me wherever you are

Lucky Star

BEFORE YOU START

Materials
– Jarol Heritage DK –Yarn A: 6(7) balls in Airforce shade 105; Yarn B: 1 ball of Anchor Artiste Metallic in Silver shade 301
– A pair of 3.25mm (US 3) knitting needles
– A pair of 4mm (US 6) knitting needles
– A set of 3.25mm (US 3) circular needles, 40cm (16in) long; (optional for working neckband in the round)
– Two stitch holders
– Tapestry needle

Sizes
S/M – To fit chest 86.5–91.5cm (34–36in), actual measurement 94cm (37in)
M/L – To fit chest 96.5–102cm (38–40in), actual measurement 108cm (42.5in)

Tension
22 sts and 28 rows to 10cm (4in) in stocking stitch on 4mm needles. Take time to check your tension and adjust as necessary to ensure an accurate fit.

SWEATER

Back
With 3.25mm needles and yarn A, cast on 98(110) sts.
Row 1 (RS): [K1, p1] rep to end. This row sets rib.
Work a further 14(14) rows in rib.
Next row (WS): Work as set in rib and **at the same time** inc 7(11) sts evenly across the row. 105(121) sts *
Change to 4mm needles and starting with a k row, work in St-st until your work measures approx. 58(63)cm / 23(25)in from cast-on edge ending with a WS row.

Shape shoulders
Next row (RS): Cast off 35(42) sts, k35(37), cast off 35(42) sts and place remaining sts on hold.

Front
Work as for Back to * then cont as follows:
Change to 4mm needles and starting with a k row, work 20(28) rows in St-st or until your work measures approx. 13(16)cm / 5(6) in from cast-on edge ending with a WS row.

Commence chart:
Note: Hold yarn B double throughout.
Row 1 (RS): With A, k19(27), join B and k1(1), with A, k11(11), with B, k1(1) with A, k to end.
Row 2 (WS): With A, p73(81), with B, p2(2), with A, p9(9), with B, p2(2), with A, p to end.
Cont as set until row 90 of chart is complete.
Cont with A only and work 12(18) rows in St-st, or until your work measures approx. 49(54)cm / 19(21½)in from cast-on edge, ending with a WS row.

Shape neck
Next row (RS): K43(50), turn your work so WS is facing, dec 1 st, p to end, turn. Cont on these sts, leaving remaining sts on hold.
** Dec 1 st at neck edge every row until 40(47) sts remain, then dec 1 st every other row until 35(42) sts remain.
Work 11(11) rows straight in St-st and cast off. ***

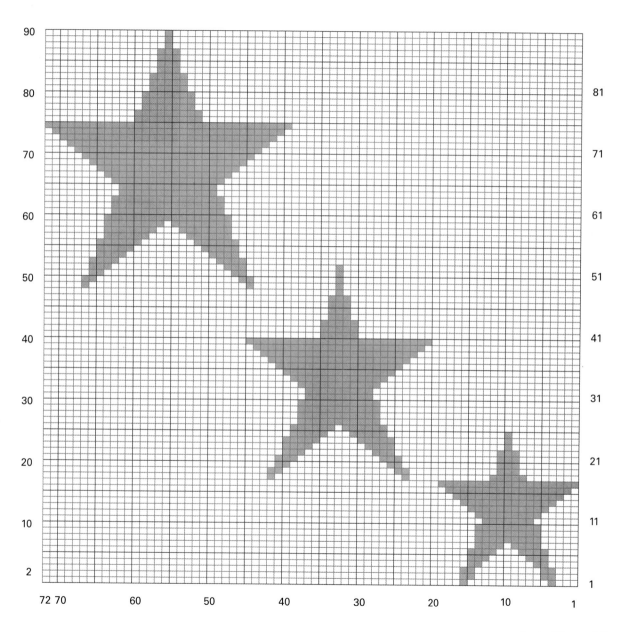

With RS facing, rejoin yarn at neck edge and k19(21), then slip these sts to holder for neckband and k to end of row.
Work as RH side from ** to ***.

Sleeves (make two)
With 3.25mm needles and yarn A, cast on 48(52) sts.
Row 1 (RS): [K1, p1] rep to end.
This row sets rib.
Work a further 14 rows in rib.
Next row (WS): Work as set in rib and **at the same time** inc 7(7) sts evenly across the row. 55(59) sts
Change to 4mm needles and starting with a k row, work in St-st and **at the same time** inc 1 st at each end of every sixth row a total of 11(13) times.
77(85) sts
Cont straight in St-st until your work measures approx. 51(56)cm / 20(22)in from cast-on edge.
Cast off loosely.

Neckband
You can do this in one of two ways depending on your preference:

Using straight needles: Join Front and Back pieces at RH shoulder. Using a 3.25mm needle and A, beginning at LH shoulder with RS facing, pick up and k28(28) sts down LH front, work 19(21) held sts, pick up and k28(28) sts up RH side, work 35(37) held sts. 106(110) sts
Work in k1, p1 rib for 7 rows, knit 1 row, work rib for 7 rows.
Cast off loosely in rib.

Using circular needles: Join both shoulder seams. With 3.25mm needle and A, beginning at LH shoulder with RS facing, pick up and k26(26) sts down LH front, work 19(21) held sts, pick up and k26(26) sts up RH side, work 35(37) held sts. 104(108) sts

Join for working in the round placing a marker to indicate beginning of round, work k1, p1 rib for 7 rounds, purl 1 round, work rib for 7 rounds.
Cast off loosely in rib.

Making up
If using straight needles join LH shoulder.
Turn garment inside out so WS is facing, fold neckband over and loosely stitch into place on WS and so it does not pull tight.
Lay garment out flat, pin sleeves into position with centre point of cast-off edge lined up to shoulder seam and stitch into place.
Join side and sleeve seams.
Gently block to measurements shown on page 8.

Picture This

Picture this: freezing cold weather

Picture This

BEFORE YOU START

Materials

– Jarol Heritage DK – Yarn A: 5(6) balls of Pink shade 109; 1 ball each in Yarn B: Winter White shade 139; Yarn C: Gold shade 140; Yarn D: Lime shade 137; Yarn E: Chilli shade 142; Yarn F: Kingfisher shade 140; Yarn G: Chocolate shade 118; Yarn H: Black shade 112
– A pair of 3.25mm (US 3) knitting needles
– A pair of 4mm (US 6) knitting needles
– A set of 3.25mm (US 3) circular needles, 40cm (16in) long; (optional for working neckband in the round)
– Two stitch holders
– Tapestry needle

Sizes

S/M – To fit chest 86.5–91.5cm (34–36in), actual measurement 94cm (37in)
M/L – To fit chest 96.5–102cm (38–40in), actual measurement 108cm (42.5in)

Tension

22 sts and 28 rows to 10cm (4in) in stocking stitch on 4mm needles. Take time to check your tension and adjust as necessary to ensure an accurate fit.

SWEATER

Back

With 3.25mm needles and yarn A, cast on 98(110) sts.
Row 1 (RS): [K1, p1] rep to end. This row sets rib.
Work a further 14(14) rows in rib.
Next row (WS): Work as set in rib and **at the same time** inc 7(11) sts evenly across the row. 105(121) sts *
Change to 4mm needles and starting with a k row, work in St-st until your work measures approx. 58(63)cm / 23(25)in from cast-on edge ending with a WS row.

Shape shoulders

Next row (RS): Cast off 35(42) sts, k35(37), cast off 35(42) sts and place remaining sts on hold.

Front

Work as for Back to * then cont as follows:
Change to 4mm needles and starting with a k row work 40(48) rows in St-st or until your work measures approx. 20(23)cm / 8(9) in from cast-on edge ending with a WS row.

Commence chart:

Note: Yarn A, the background colour, is not shown on the chart; yarn B is the start of the white frame area.
Row 1 (RS): With A, k30(38), join B and k45(45), with A, k to end.
Row 2 (WS): With A, p30(38), with B, p45(45), with A, p to end.
Cont as set until row 65 of chart is complete.
Cont with A only and starting with a WS p row, work 17(23) rows in St-st, or until your work measures approx. 49(54)cm / 19(21½)in from cast-on edge, ending with a WS row.

Shape neck

Next row (RS): K43(50), turn your work so WS is facing, dec 1 st, p to end, turn. Cont on these sts, leaving remaining sts on hold.
**** Dec 1 st at neck edge every row until 40(47) sts remain, then dec 1 st every other row until 35(42) sts remain.
Work 11(11) rows straight in St-st and cast off. *****
With RS facing, rejoin yarn at neck edge and k19(21), then slip these sts to holder for neckband and k to end of row.
Work as RH side from ** to ***.

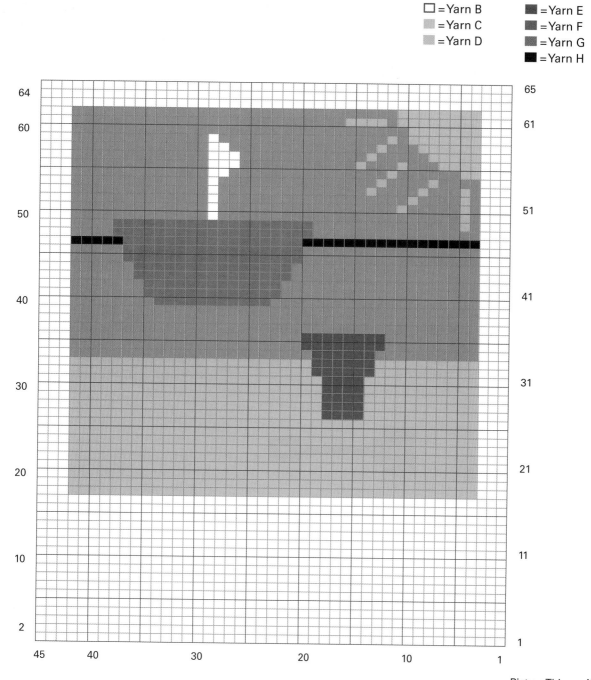

=Yarn B
=Yarn C
=Yarn D
=Yarn E
=Yarn F
=Yarn G
=Yarn H

Sleeves (make two)

With 3.25mm needles and yarn A, cast on 48(52) sts.

Row 1 (RS): [K1, p1] rep to end. This row sets rib.

Work a further 14 rows in rib.

Next row (WS): Work as set in rib and **at the same time** inc 7(7) sts evenly across the row. 55(59) sts

Change to 4mm needles and starting with a k row, work in St-st and **at the same time** inc 1 st at each end of every sixth row a total of 11(13) times. 77(85) sts

Cont straight in St-st until your work measures approx. 51(56)cm / 20(22)in from cast-on edge.

Cast off loosely.

Neckband

You can do this in one of two ways depending on your preference:

Using straight needles: Join Front and Back pieces at RH shoulder. Using a 3.25mm needle and A, beginning at LH shoulder with RS facing, pick up and k28(28) sts down LH front, work 19(21) held sts, pick up and k28(28) sts up RH side, work 35(37) held sts. 106(110) sts

Work in k1, p1 rib for 7 rows, knit 1 row, work rib for 7 rows. Cast off loosely in rib.

Using circular needles: Join both shoulder seams. With 3.25mm needle and A, beginning at LH shoulder with RS facing, pick up and k26(26) sts down LH front, work 19(21) held sts, pick up and k26(26) sts up RH side, work 35(37) held sts. 104(108) sts

Join for working in the round placing a marker to indicate beginning of round, work k1, p1 rib for 7 rounds, purl 1 round, work rib for 7 rounds. Cast off loosely in rib.

Making up

If using straight needles join LH shoulder.

Turn garment inside out so WS is facing, fold neckband over and loosely stitch into place on WS and so it does not pull tight.

Lay garment out flat, pin sleeves into position with centre point of cast-off edge lined up to shoulder seam and stitch into place.

Join side and sleeve seams. Gently block to measurements shown on page 8.

Me Jane

Good lord, it's me Jane

Me Jane

BEFORE YOU START

Materials
– Jarol Heritage DK – Yarn A: 5(6) balls in Black shade 112; 1 ball each in Yarn B: Camel shade 103; Yarn C: Chocolate shade 118
– A pair of 3.25mm (US 3) knitting needles
– A pair of 4mm (US 6) knitting needles
– A set of 3.25mm (US 3) circular needles, 40cm (16in) long; (optional for working neckband in the round)
– Two stitch holders
– Tapestry needle

Sizes
S/M – To fit chest 86.5–91.5cm (34–36in), actual measurement 94cm (37in)
M/L – To fit chest 96.5–102cm (38–40in), actual measurement 108cm (42.5in)

Tension
22 sts and 28 rows to 10cm (4in) in stocking stitch on 4mm needles. Take time to check your tension and adjust as necessary to ensure an accurate fit.

SWEATER

Back
With 3.25mm needles and yarn A, cast on 98(110) sts.
Row 1 (RS): [K1, p1] rep to end.
This row sets rib.
Work a further 14(14) rows in rib.
Next row (WS): Work as set in rib and **at the same time** inc 7(11) sts evenly across the row. 105(121) sts *
Change to 4mm needles and starting with a k row, work in St-st until your work measures approx. 58(63)cm / 23(25)in from cast-on edge ending with a WS row.

Shape shoulders
Next row (RS): Cast off 35(42) sts, k35(37), cast off 35(42) sts and place remaining sts on hold.

Front
Work as for Back to * then cont as follows:
Change to 4mm needles and starting with a k row, work 14(20) rows in St-st or until your work measures approx. 11(13)cm / 4¼(5)in from cast-on edge ending with a WS row.

Commence chart:
Row 1 (RS): With A, k47(54), join B and k12(12), with A, k to end.
Row 2 (WS): With A, p42(51), using B, p20(20), with A, p to end.
Cont as set until row 96 of chart is complete.
Cont with A only and work 12(20) rows in St-st, or until your work measures approx. 49(54)cm / 19(21½)in from cast-on edge, ending with a WS row.

Shape neck
Next row (RS): K43(50), turn your work so WS is facing, dec 1 st, p to end, turn. Cont on these sts, leaving remaining sts on hold.
** Dec 1 st at neck edge every row until 40(47) sts remain, then dec 1 st every other row until 35(42) sts remain.
Work 11(11) rows straight in St-st and cast off. ***
With RS facing, rejoin yarn at neck edge and k19(21), then slip these sts to holder for neckband and k to end of row.
Work as RH side from ** to ***.

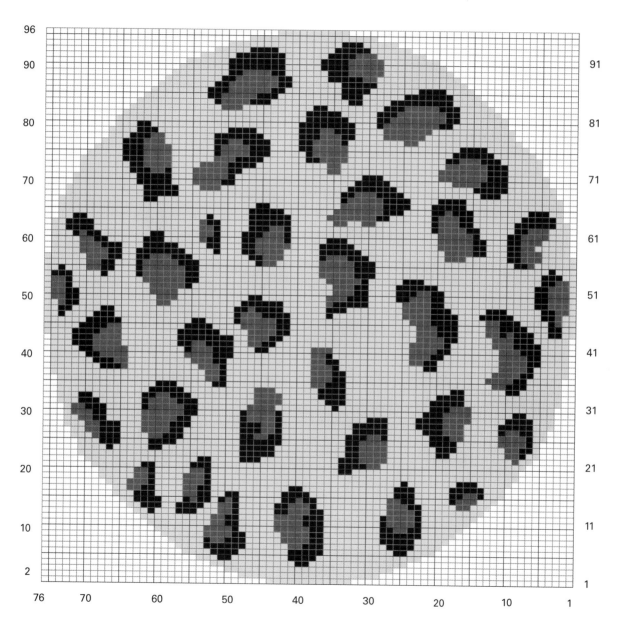

Sleeves (make two)

With 3.25mm needles and yarn A, cast on 48(52) sts.

Row 1 (RS): [K1, p1] rep to end. This row sets rib.

Work a further 14 rows in rib.

Next row (WS): Work as set in rib and **at the same time** inc 7(7) sts evenly across the row. 55(59) sts

Change to 4mm needles and starting with a k row, work in St-st and **at the same time** inc 1 st at each end of every sixth row a total of 11(13) times. 77(85) sts

Cont straight in St-st until your work measures approx. 51(56)cm / 20(22)in from cast-on edge.

Cast off loosely.

Neckband

You can do this in one of two ways depending on your preference:

Using straight needles: Join Front and Back pieces at RH shoulder. Using a 3.25mm needle and A, beginning at LH shoulder with RS facing, pick up and k28(28) sts down LH front, work 19(21) held sts, pick up and k28(28) sts up RH side, work 35(37) held sts. 106(110) sts

Work in k1, p1 rib for 7 rows, knit 1 row, work rib for 7 rows. Cast off loosely in rib.

Using circular needles: Join both shoulder seams. With 3.25mm needle and A, beginning at LH shoulder with RS facing, pick up and k26(26) sts down LH front, work 19(21) held sts, pick up and k26(26) sts up RH side, work 35(37) held sts 104(108) sts

Join for working in the round placing a marker to indicate beginning of round, work k1, p1 rib for 7 rounds, purl 1 round, work rib for 7 rounds. Cast off loosely in rib.

Making up

If using straight needles join LH shoulder.

Turn garment inside out so WS is facing, fold neckband over and loosely stitch into place on WS and so it does not pull tight.

Lay garment out flat, pin sleeves into position with centre point of cast-off edge lined up to shoulder seam and stitch into place.

Join side and sleeve seams. Gently block to measurements shown on page 8.

Mr Moustache

Fill me in on your new vision

Mr Moustache

Materials

– Jarol Heritage DK – Yarn A: 6(7)
balls in Cream shade 100; Yarn B;
1 ball in Black shade 112
– A pair of 3.25mm (US 3)
knitting needles
– A pair of 4mm (US 6)
knitting needles
A set of 3.25mm (US 3) circular
– needles, 40cm (16in) long;
(optional for working neckband
in the round)
– Two stitch holders
– Tapestry needle

Sizes

S/M – To fit chest 86.5–91.5cm
(34–36in), actual measurement
94cm (37in)
M/L – To fit chest 96.5–102cm
(38–40in), actual measurement
108cm (42.5in)

Tension

22 sts and 28 rows to 10cm
(4in) in stocking stitch on 4mm
needles. Take time to check your
tension and adjust as necessary
to ensure an accurate fit.

SWEATER

Back

With 3.25mm needles and yarn A,
cast on 98(110) sts.
Row 1 (RS): [K1, p1] rep to end.
This row sets rib.
Work a further 14(14) rows in rib.
Next row (WS): Work as set in
rib and **at the same time** inc
7(11) sts evenly across the row.
105(121) sts *
Change to 4mm needles and
starting with a k row, work in
St-st until your work measures
approx. 58(63)cm / 23(25)in
from cast-on edge ending with
a WS row.

Shape shoulders

Next row (RS): Cast off 35(42) sts,
k35(37), cast off 35(42) sts and
place remaining sts on hold.

Front

Work as for Back to * then cont as
follows:
Change to 4mm needles and
starting with a k row work 68(76)
rows in St-st or until your work
measures approx. 11(13)cm /
4¼(5)in from cast-on edge ending
with a WS row.

Commence chart:

Row 1 (RS): With A, k27(35), join
B and k9(9), with A, k33(33),
with B, k9(9), with A, k to end.
Row 2 (WS): With A, p22(30),
with B, p18(18), with A, p25(25),
with B, p18(18), with A, p to end.
Cont as set until row 26 of chart
is complete.
Cont with A only and work 28(34)
rows in St-st, or until your work
measures approx. 49(54)cm /
19(21½)in from cast-on edge,
ending with a WS row.

Shape neck

Next row (RS): K43(50), turn your
work so WS is facing, dec 1 st, p
to end, turn. Cont on these sts,
leaving remaining sts on hold.
** Dec 1 st at neck edge every
row until 40(47) sts remain, then
dec 1 st every other row until
35(42) sts remain.
Work 11(11) rows straight in St-st
and cast off. ***
With RS facing, rejoin yarn at
neck edge and k19(21), then slip
these sts to holder for neckband
and k to end of row.
Work as RH side from ** to ***.

= Yarn A
= Yarn B

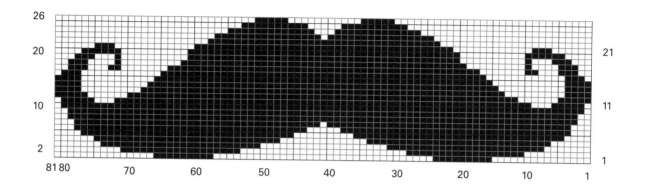

Sleeves (make two)

With 3.25mm needles and yarn A, cast on 48(52) sts.

Row 1 (RS): [K1, p1] rep to end. This row sets rib.

Work a further 14 rows in rib.

Next row (WS): Work as set in rib and **at the same time** inc 7(7) sts evenly across the row. 55(59) sts

Change to 4mm needles and starting with a k row, work in St-st and **at the same time** inc 1 st at each end of every sixth row a total of 11(13) times. 77(85) sts

Cont straight in St-st until your work measures approx. 51(56)cm / 20(22)in from cast-on edge.

Cast off loosely.

Neckband

You can do this in one of two ways depending on your preference:

Using straight needles: Join Front and Back pieces at RH shoulder. Using a 3.25mm needle and A, beginning at LH shoulder with RS facing, pick up and k28(28) sts down LH front, work 19(21) held sts, pick up and k28(28) sts up RH side, work 35(37) held sts. 106(110) sts

Work in k1, p1 rib for 7 rows, knit 1 row, work rib for 7 rows.

Cast off loosely in rib.

Using circular needles: Join both shoulder seams. With 3.25mm needle and A, beginning at LH shoulder with RS facing, pick up and k26(26) sts down LH front, work 19(21) held sts, pick up and k26(26) sts up RH side, work 35(37) held sts. 104(108) sts

Join for working in the round placing a marker to indicate beginning of round, work k1, p1 rib for 7 rounds, purl 1 round, work rib for 7 rounds.

Cast off loosely in rib.

Making up

If using straight needles join LH shoulder.

Turn garment inside out so WS is facing, fold neckband over and loosely stitch into place on WS and so it does not pull tight.

Lay garment out flat, pin sleeves into position with centre point of cast-off edge lined up to shoulder seam and stitch into place.

Join side and sleeve seams.

Gently block to measurements shown on page 8.

Paint It Black

*No colours any more, I want
them to turn black*

Paint It Black

Materials
– Jarol Heritage DK – Yarn A: 2(3) balls in Chilli shade 142; Yarn B: 3(4) balls in Black shade 112
– One pair of 3.25mm (US 3) knitting needles
– A pair of 4mm (US 6) knitting needles
– A set of 3.25mm (US 3) circular needles, 40cm (16in) long; (optional for working neckband in the round)
– Two stitch holders
– Tapestry needle

Sizes
S/M – To fit chest 86.5–91.5cm (34–36in), actual measurement 94cm (37in)
M/L – To fit chest 96.5–102cm (38–40in), actual measurement 108cm (42.5in)

Tension
22 sts and 28 rows to 10cm (4in) in stocking stitch on 4mm needles. Take time to check your tension and adjust as necessary to ensure an accurate fit.

SWEATER

Back
With 3.25mm needles and yarn A, cast on 98(110) sts.
Row 1 (RS): [K1, p1] rep to end. This row sets rib.
Work a further 14(14) rows in rib.
Next row (WS): Work as set in rib and **at the same time** inc 7(11) sts evenly across the row. 105(121) sts *
Change to 4mm needles and starting with a k row, work in St-st until your work measures approx. 58(63)cm / 23(25)in from cast-on edge ending with a WS row.

Shape shoulders
Next row (RS): Cast off 35(42) sts, k35(37), cast off 35(42) sts and place remaining sts on hold.

Front
Work as for Back to * then cont as follows:
Change to 4mm needles and starting with a k row work 20(30) rows in St-st or until your work measures approx. 13(16.5)cm / 5(6½)in from cast-on edge ending with a WS row.

Commence chart:
Note: Work S/M up to first red line on chart; work M/L up to second red line on chart.
Row 1 (RS): With A k22(24), with B, k2(2), with A, k38(38), with B, k2(2), with A, k to end.
Row 2 (WS): With A, p36(49), with B, p4(4), with A, p42(42), with B, p3(3), with A, p to end.
Cont as set until row 50 of chart is complete.
Cont with B only and work 52(56) rows in St-st, or until your work measures approx. 49(54)cm / 19(21½)in from cast-on edge, ending with a WS row.

Shape neck
Next row (RS): K43(50), turn your work so WS is facing, dec 1 st, p to end, turn. Cont on these sts, leaving remaining sts on hold.
**** Dec 1 st at neck edge every row until 40(47) sts remain, then dec 1 st every other row until 35(42) sts remain.
Work 11(11) rows straight in St-st and cast off. ***
With RS facing, rejoin yarn at neck edge and k19(21), then slip these sts to holder for neckband and k to end of row.
Work as RH side from ** to ***.

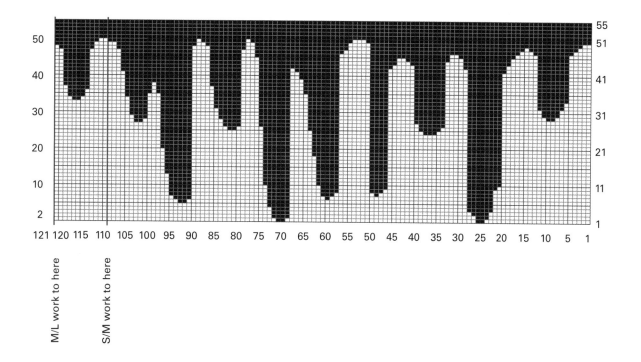

Sleeves (make two)

With 3.25mm needles and yarn B, cast on 48(52) sts.

Row 1 (RS): [K1, p1] rep to end. This row sets rib.

Work a further 14 rows in rib.

Next row (WS): Work as set in rib and **at the same time** inc 7(7) sts evenly across the row. 55(59) sts

Change to 4mm needles and starting with a k row, work in St-st and **at the same time** inc 1 st at each end of every sixth row a total of 11(13) times. 77(85) sts.

Cont straight in St-st until your work measures approx. 51(56)cm / 20(22)in from cast-on edge.

Cast off loosely.

Neckband

You can do this in one of two ways depending on your preference:

Using straight needles: Join Front and Back pieces at RH shoulder. Using a 3.25mm needle and B, beginning at LH shoulder with RS facing, pick up and k28(28) sts down LH front, work 19(21) held sts, pick up and k28(28) sts up RH side, work 35(37) held sts. 106(110) sts

Work in k1, p1 rib for 7 rows, knit 1 row, work rib for 7 rows.

Cast off loosely in rib.

Using circular needles: Join both shoulder seams. With 3.25mm needle and B, beginning at LH shoulder with RS facing, pick up and k26(26) sts down LH front, work 19(21) held sts, pick up and k26(26) sts up RH side, work 35(37) held sts. 104(108) sts

Join for working in the round placing a marker to indicate beginning of round, work k1, p1 rib for 7 rounds, purl 1 round, work rib for 7 rounds.

Cast off loosely in rib.

Making up

If using straight needles join LH shoulder.

Turn garment inside out so WS is facing, fold neckband over and loosely stitch into place on WS and so it does not pull tight.

Lay garment out flat, pin sleeves into position with centre point of cast-off edge lined up to shoulder seam and stitch into place.

Join side and sleeve seams.

Gently block to measurements shown on page 8.

Spring

Don't you realise we're two of a kind

Spring

BEFORE YOU START

Materials
– Jarol Heritage DK – Yarn A: 5(6) balls in Silver Grey shade 134; 1 ball each in Yarn B: Chilli shade 142; Yarn C: Kingfisher shade 136; Yarn D: Cerise shade 133; Yarn E: Lime shade 137
– A pair of 3.25mm (US 3) knitting needles
– A pair of 4mm (US 6) knitting needles
– A set of 3.25mm (US 3) circular needles, 40cm (16in) long; (optional for working neckband in the round)
– Two stitch holders
– Tapestry needle

Sizes
S/M – To fit chest 86.5–91.5cm (34–36in), actual measurement 94cm (37in)
M/L – To fit chest 96.5–102cm (38–40in), actual measurement 108cm (42.5in)

Tension
22 sts and 28 rows to 10cm (4in) in stocking stitch on 4mm needles. Take time to check your tension and adjust as necessary to ensure an accurate fit.

SWEATER

Back
With 3.25mm needles and yarn A, cast on 98(110) sts.
Row 1 (RS): [K1, p1] rep to end. This row sets rib.
Work a further 14(14) rows in rib.
Next row (WS): Work as set in rib and **at the same time** inc 7(11) sts evenly across the row. 105(121) sts *
Change to 4mm needles and starting with a k row, work in St-st until your work measures approx. 58(63)cm / 23(25)in from cast-on edge ending with a WS row.

Shape shoulders
Next row (RS): Cast off 35(42) sts, k35(37), cast off 35(42) sts and place remaining sts on hold.

Front
Work as for Back to * then cont as follows:
Change to 4mm needles and starting with a k row work 2(10) rows in St-st.

Commence chart:
Row 1 (RS): With A, k22(30) join B, k5(5), with A, k to end.
Row 2 (WS): With A, p76(84), using B, p9(9), with A, p to end.
Cont as set until row 117 of chart is complete.
Cont with A only and starting with a WS p row, work 3(9) rows in St-st, or until your work measures approx. 49(54)cm / 19(21½)in from cast-on edge, ending with a WS row.

Shape neck
Next row (RS): K43(50), turn your work so WS is facing, dec 1 st, p to end, turn. Cont on these sts, leaving remaining sts on hold.
** Dec 1 st at neck edge every row until 40(47) sts remain, then dec 1 st every other row until 35(42) sts remain.
Work 11(11) rows straight in St-st and cast off. ***
With RS facing, rejoin yarn at neck edge and k19(21), then slip these sts to holder for neckband and k to end of row.
Work as RH side from ** to ***.

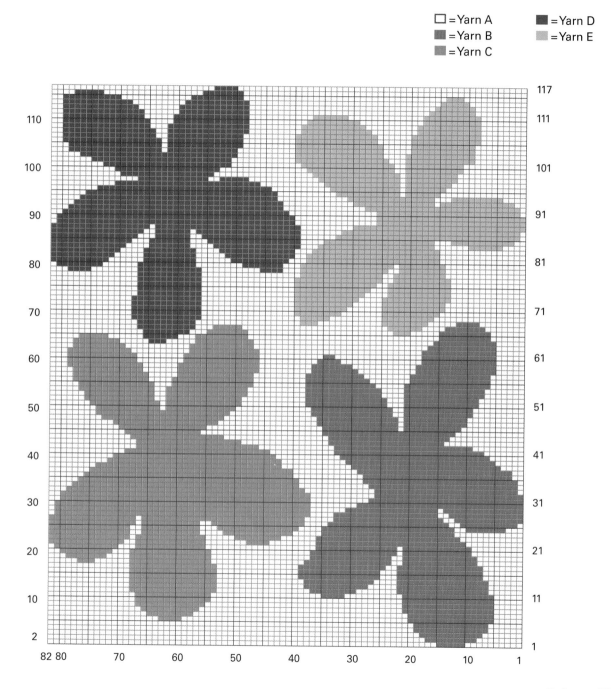

Sleeves (make two)

With 3.25mm needles and yarn A, cast on 48(52) sts.

Row 1 (RS): [K1, p1] rep to end. This row sets rib.

Work a further 14 rows in rib.

Next row (WS): Work as set in rib and **at the same time** inc 7(7) sts evenly across the row. 55(59) sts Change to 4mm needles and starting with a k row, work in St-st and **at the same time** inc 1 st at each end of every sixth row a total of 11(13) times. 77(85) sts.

Cont straight in St-st until your work measures approx. 51(56)cm / 20(22)in from cast-on edge.

Cast off loosely.

Neckband

You can do this in one of two ways depending on your preference:

Using straight needles: Join Front and Back pieces at RH shoulder. Using a 3.25mm needle and A, beginning at LH shoulder with RS facing, pick up and k28(28) sts down LH front, work 19(21) held sts, pick up and k28(28) sts up RH side, work 35(37) held sts. 106(110) sts Work in k1, p1 rib for 7 rows, knit 1 row, work rib for 7 rows. Cast off loosely in rib.

Using circular needles: Join both shoulder seams. With 3.25mm needle and A, beginning at LH shoulder with RS facing, pick up and k26(26) sts down LH front, work 19(21) held sts, pick up and k26(26) sts up RH side, work 35(37) held sts. 104(108) sts

Join for working in the round placing a marker to indicate beginning of round, work k1, p1 rib for 7 rounds, purl 1 round, work rib for 7 rounds. Cast off loosely in rib.

Making up

If using straight needles join LH shoulder.

Turn garment inside out so WS is facing, fold neckband over and loosely stitch into place on WS and so it does not pull tight. Lay garment out flat, pin sleeves into position with centre point of cast-off edge lined up to shoulder seam and stitch into place.

Join side and sleeve seams. Gently block to measurements shown on page 8.

On Repeat

Beats on repeat, beating on me

On Repeat

BEFORE YOU START

Materials
– Jarol Heritage DK – Yarn A: 6(7)
balls in Black shade 112; Yarn B:
1 ball in Winter White shade 139
– A pair of 3.25mm (US 3)
knitting needles
– A pair of 4mm (US 6)
knitting needles
– A set of 3.25mm (US 3) circular
needles, 40cm (16in) long;
(optional for working neckband
in the round)
– Two stitch holders
– Tapestry needle

Sizes
S/M – To fit chest 86.5–91.5cm
(34–36in), actual measurement
94cm (37in)
M/L – To fit chest 96.5–102cm
(38–40in), actual measurement
108cm (42.5in)

Tension
22 sts and 28 rows to 10cm
(4in) in stocking stitch on 4mm
needles. Take time to check your
tension and adjust as necessary
to ensure an accurate fit.

SWEATER

Back
With 3.25mm needles and yarn A,
cast on 98(110) sts.
Row 1 (RS): [K1, p1] rep to end.
This row sets rib.
Work a further 14(14) rows in rib.
Next row (WS): Work as set in
rib and **at the same time** inc
7(11) sts evenly across the row.
105(121) sts *
Change to 4mm needles and
starting with a k row, work in
St-st until your work measures
approx. 58(63)cm / 23(25)in
from cast-on edge ending with
a WS row.

Shape shoulders
Next row (RS): Cast off 35(42) sts,
k35(37), cast off 35(42) sts and
place remaining sts on hold.

Front
Work as for Back to * then cont
as follows:
Change to 4mm needle, yarn B
and starting with k row work 2
rows in St-st.
Change to A and work 4 rows in
St-st.

Commence chart:
Row 1 (RS): With A, k4(4), k red
boxed repeat 6(7) times changing
colour as indicated, with A, k to
end.
Row 2 (WS): With A, p5(5), p red
boxed repeat 6(7) times changing
colour as indicated, with A, p to
end.
Cont as set until row 36 of chart
is complete.
Cont with A only and work 80(94)
rows in St-st, or until your work
measures approx. 49(54)cm /
19(21½)in from cast-on edge,
ending with a WS row.

Shape neck
Next row (RS): K43(50), turn your
work so WS is facing, dec 1 st,
p to end, turn. Cont on these sts,
leaving remaining sts on hold.
** Dec 1 st at neck edge every
row until 40(47) sts remain, then
dec 1 st every other row until
35(42) sts remain.
Work 11(11) rows straight in St-st
and cast off. ***
With RS facing, rejoin yarn at
neck edge and k19(21), then slip
these sts to holder for neckband
and k to end of row.
Work as RH side from ** to ***.

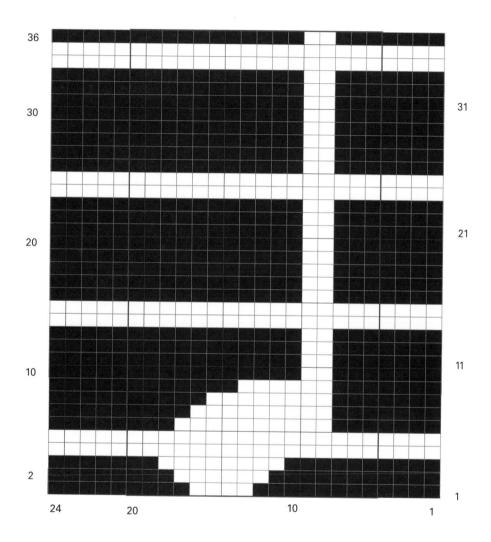

36

30

31

20

21

10

11

2

1

24

20

10

1

Sleeves (make two)

With 3.25mm needles and yarn A, cast on 48(52) sts.

Row 1 (RS): [K1, p1] rep to end. This row sets rib.

Work a further 14 rows in rib.

Next row (WS): Work as set in rib and **at the same time** inc 7(7) sts evenly across the row. 55(59) sts

Change to 4mm needles and starting with a k row, work in St-st and **at the same time** inc 1 st at each end of every sixth row a total of 11(13) times. 77(85) sts.

Cont straight in St-st until your work measures approx. 51(56)cm / 20(22)in from cast-on edge.

Cast off loosely.

Neckband

You can do this in one of two ways depending on your preference:

Using straight needles: Join Front and Back pieces at RH shoulder. Using a 3.25mm needle and A, beginning at LH shoulder with RS facing, pick up and k28(28) sts down LH front, work 19(21) held sts, pick up and k28(28) sts up RH side, work 35(37) held sts. 106(110) sts Work in k1, p1 rib for 7 rows, knit 1 row, work rib for 7 rows. Cast off loosely in rib.

Using circular needles: Join both shoulder seams. With 3.25mm needle and A, beginning at LH shoulder with RS facing, pick up and k26(26) sts down LH front, work 19(21) held sts, pick up and k26(26) sts up RH side, work 35(37) held sts. 104(108) sts

Join for working in the round placing a marker to indicate beginning of round, work k1, p1 rib for 7 rounds, purl 1 round, work rib for 7 rounds. Cast off loosely in rib.

Making up

If using straight needles join LH shoulder.

Turn garment inside out so WS is facing, fold neckband over and loosely stitch into place on WS and so it does not pull tight.

Lay garment out flat, pin sleeves into position with centre point of cast-off edge lined up to shoulder seam and stitch into place.

Join side and sleeve seams. Gently block to measurements shown on page 8.

Telephone

*Call all you want, but
there's no one home*

Telephone

BEFORE YOU START

Materials
– Jarol Heritage DK – Yarn A: 6(7) balls in Chilli shade 142; Yarn B: 1 ball in Gold shade 140
– A pair of 3.25mm (US 3) knitting needles
– A pair of 4mm (US 6) knitting needles
– A set of 3.25mm (US 3) circular needles, 40cm (16in) long; (optional for working neckband in the round)
– Two stitch holders
– Tapestry needle

Sizes
S/M – To fit chest 86.5–91.5cm (34–36in), actual measurement 94cm (37in)
M/L – To fit chest 96.5–102cm (38–40in), actual measurement 108cm (42.5in)

Tension
22 sts and 28 rows to 10cm (4in) in stocking stitch on 4mm needles. Take time to check your tension and adjust as necessary to ensure an accurate fit.

SWEATER

Back
With 3.25mm needles and yarn A, cast on 98(110) sts.
Row 1 (RS): [K1, p1] rep to end.
This row sets rib.
Work a further 14(14) rows in rib.
Next row (WS): Work as set in rib and **at the same time** inc 7(11) sts evenly across the row. 105(121) sts *
Change to 4mm needles and starting with a k row, work in St-st until your work measures approx. 58(63)cm / 23(25)in from cast-on edge ending with a WS row.

Shape shoulders
Next row (RS): Cast off 35(42) sts, k35(37), cast off 35(42) sts and place remaining sts on hold.

Front
Work as for Back to * then cont as follows:
Change to 4mm needles and starting with a k row work 20(30) rows in St-st or until your work measures approx. 13(16.5)cm / 5(6½)in from cast-on edge ending with a WS row.

Commence chart:
Row 1 (RS): With A, k54(64), join B and k5(5), with A, k to end.
Row 2 (WS): With A, p45(51), using B, p7(7), with A, p to end.
Cont as set until row 85 of chart is complete.
Cont with A only and starting with a WS p row, work 17(21) rows in St-st, or until your work measures approx. 49(54)cm / 19(21½)in from cast-on edge, ending with a WS row.

Shape neck
Next row (RS): K43(50), turn your work so WS is facing, dec 1 st, p to end, turn. Cont on these sts, leaving remaining sts on hold.
** Dec 1 st at neck edge every row until 40(47) sts remain, then dec 1 st every other row until 35(42) sts remain.
Work 11(11) rows straight in St-st and cast off. ***
With RS facing, rejoin yarn at neck edge and k19(21), then slip these sts to holder for neckband and k to end of row.
Work as RH side from ** to ***.

□ = Yarn A
▨ = Yarn B

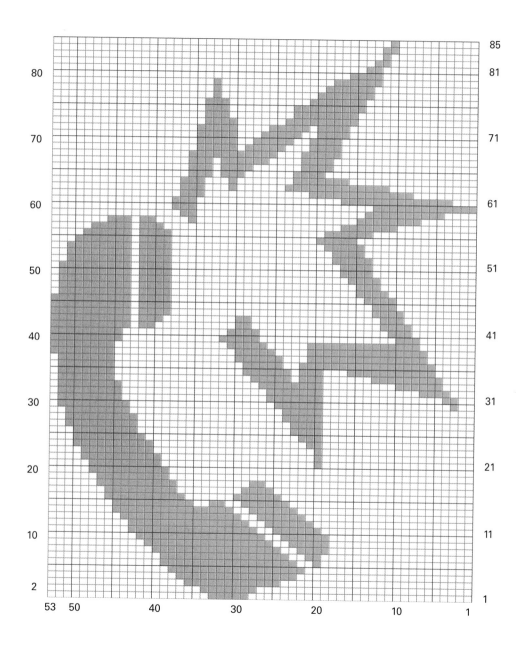

Sleeves (make two)

With 3.25mm needles and yarn A, cast on 48(52) sts.

Row 1 (RS): [K1, p1] rep to end. This row sets rib.

Work a further 14 rows in rib.

Next row (WS): Work as set in rib and **at the same time** inc 7(7) sts evenly across the row. 55(59) sts

Change to 4mm needles and starting with a k row, work in St-st and **at the same time** inc 1 st at each end of every sixth row a total of 11(13) times. 77(85) sts.

Cont straight in St-st until your work measures approx. 51(56)cm / 20(22)in from cast-on edge.

Cast off loosely.

Neckband

You can do this in one of two ways depending on your preference:

Using straight needles: Join Front and Back pieces at RH shoulder. Using a 3.25mm needle and A, beginning at LH shoulder with RS facing, pick up and k28(28) sts down LH front, work 19(21) held sts, pick up and k28(28) sts up RH side, work 35(37) held sts. 106(110) sts Work in k1, p1 rib for 7 rows, knit 1 row, work rib for 7 rows. Cast off loosely in rib.

Using circular needles: Join both shoulder seams. With 3.25mm needle and A, beginning at LH shoulder with RS facing, pick up and k26(26) sts down LH front, work 19(21) held sts, pick up and k26(26) sts up RH side, work 35(37) held sts. 104(108) sts

Join for working in the round placing a marker to indicate beginning of round, work k1, p1 rib for 7 rounds, purl 1 round, work rib for 7 rounds. Cast off loosely in rib.

Making up

If using straight needles join LH shoulder.

Turn garment inside out so WS is facing, fold neckband over and loosely stitch into place on WS and so it does not pull tight.

Lay garment out flat, pin sleeves into position with centre point of cast-off edge lined up to shoulder seam and stitch into place.

Join side and sleeve seams.

Gently block to measurements shown on page 8.

Bad Girls

Bad girls do it well

Bad Girls

BEFORE YOU START

Materials
– Jarol Heritage DK – Yarn A: 6(7) balls in Kingfisher shade 136; Yarn B: 1 ball in Gold shade 140
– A pair of 3.25mm (US 3) knitting needles
– A pair of 4mm (US 6) knitting needles
– A set of 3.25mm (US 3) circular needles, 40cm (16in) long; (optional for working neckband in the round)
– Two stitch holders
– Tapestry needle

Sizes
S/M – To fit chest 86.5–91.5cm (34–36in), actual measurement 94cm (37in)
M/L – To fit chest 96.5–102cm (38–40in), actual measurement 108cm (42.5in)

Tension
22 sts and 28 rows to 10cm (4in) in stocking stitch on 4mm needles. Take time to check your tension and adjust as necessary to ensure an accurate fit.

SWEATER

Back
With 3.25mm needles and yarn A, cast on 98(110) sts.
Row 1 (RS): [K1, p1] rep to end. This row sets rib.
Work a further 14(14) rows in rib.
Next row (WS): Work as set in rib and **at the same time** inc 7(11) sts evenly across the row. 105(121) sts *****
Change to 4mm needles and starting with a k row, work in St-st until your work measures approx. 58(63)cm / 23(25)in from cast-on edge ending with a WS row.

Shape shoulders
Next row (RS): Cast off 35(42) sts, k35(37), cast off 35(42) sts and place remaining sts on hold.

Front
Work as for Back to ***** then cont as follows:
Change to 4mm needles and starting with a k row work 28(28) rows in St-st, or until your work measures approx. 49(54)cm / 19(21½)in from cast-on edge, ending with a WS row.

Commence chart:
Row 1 (RS): With A k52(60), join B and k1, with A, k to end of row.
Row 2 (WS): With A, p51(59), with B, p2, with A, p to end.
Cont to work from chart, shaping neck at same time as follows:
Next row: K43(50) turn, dec 1 st, p to end. Work on these sts leaving remaining 62(71) sts on hold and cont as follows: Dec 1 st at neck edge every row until 40(47) sts rem, then alt rows until 35(42) sts remain.
Work 12(12) rows straight in St-st and cast off.

Shape neck
Next row (RS): K43(50), turn your work so WS is facing, dec 1 st, p to end, turn. Cont on these sts, leaving remaining sts on hold.
**Dec 1 st at neck edge every row until 40(47) sts remain, then dec 1 st every other row until 35(42) sts remain.
Work 11(11) rows straight in St-st and cast off.*******
With RS facing, rejoin yarn at neck edge and k19(21), then slip these sts to holder for neckband and k to end of row.
Work as RH side from ****** to *******.

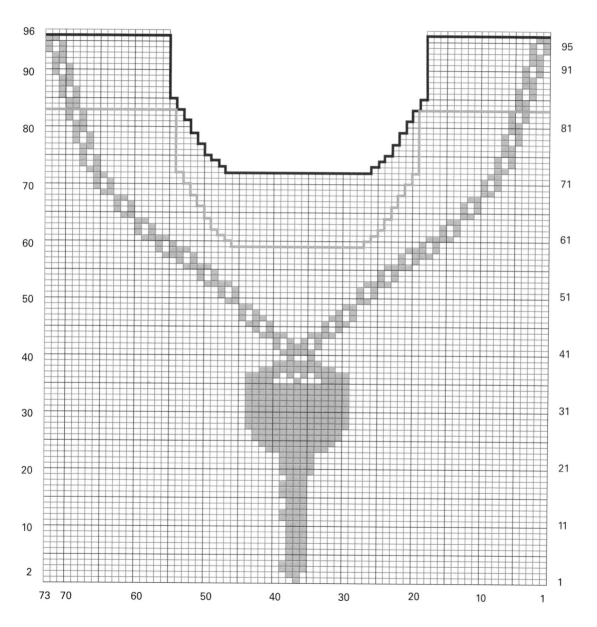

Sleeves (make two)

With 3.25mm needles and yarn A, cast on 48(52) sts.

Row 1 (RS): [K1, p1] rep to end. This row sets rib.

Work a further 14 rows in rib.

Next row (WS): Work as set in rib and **at the same time** inc 7(7) sts evenly across the row. 55(59) sts

Change to 4mm needles and starting with a k row, work in St-st and **at the same time** inc 1 st at each end of every sixth row a total of 11(13) times. 77(85) sts.

Cont straight in St-st until your work measures approx. 51(56)cm / 20(22)in from cast-on edge.

Cast off loosely.

Neckband

You can do this in one of two ways depending on your preference:

Using straight needles: Join Front and Back pieces at RH shoulder. Using a 3.25mm needle and A, beginning at LH shoulder with RS facing, pick up and k28(28) sts down LH front, work 19(21) held sts, pick up and k28(28) sts up RH side, work 35(37) held sts. 106(110) sts

Work in k1, p1 rib for 7 rows, knit 1 row, work rib for 7 rows.

Cast off loosely in rib.

Using circular needles: Join both shoulder seams. With 3.25mm needle and A, beginning at LH shoulder with RS facing, pick up and k26(26) sts down LH front, work 19(21) held sts, pick up and k26(26) sts up RH side, work 35(37) held sts. 104(108) sts

Join for working in the round placing a marker to indicate beginning of round, work k1, p1 rib for 7 rounds, purl 1 round, work rib for 7 rounds.

Cast off loosely in rib.

Making up

If using straight needles join LH shoulder.

Turn garment inside out so WS is facing, fold neckband over and loosely stitch into place on WS and so it does not pull tight.

Lay garment out flat, pin sleeves into position with centre point of cast-off edge lined up to shoulder seam and stitch into place.

Join side and sleeve seams.

Gently block to measurements shown on page 8.

Weather Experience

It'll be a fine, dry day

Weather Experience

BEFORE YOU START

Materials
– Jarol Heritage DK – Yarn A: 6(7) balls in Lime shade 137; 1 ball each in Yarn B: Winter White shade 139; Yarn C: Gold shade 140; Yarn D: Kingfisher shade 136; Yarn E: Silver Grey shade 134
– A pair of 3.25mm (US 3) knitting needles
– A pair of 4mm (US 6) knitting needles
– A set of 3.25mm (US 3) circular needles, 40cm (16in) long; (optional for working neckband in the round)
– Two stitch holders
– Tapestry needle

Sizes
S/M – To fit chest 86.5–91.5cm (34–36in), actual measurement 94cm (37in)
M/L – To fit chest 96.5–102cm (38–40in), actual measurement 108cm (42.5in)

Tension
22 sts and 28 rows to 10cm (4in) in stocking stitch on 4mm needles. Take time to check your tension and adjust as necessary to ensure an accurate fit.

SWEATER

Back
With 3.25mm needles and yarn A, cast on 98(110) sts.
Row 1 (RS): [K1, p1] rep to end. This row sets rib.
Work a further 14(14) rows in rib.
Next row (WS): Work as set in rib and **at the same time** inc 7(11) sts evenly across the row. 105(121) sts *
Change to 4mm needles and starting with a k row, work in St-st until your work measures approx. 58(63)cm / 23(25)in from cast-on edge ending with a WS row.

Shape shoulders
Next row (RS): Cast off 35(42) sts, k35(37), cast off 35(42) sts and place remaining sts on hold.

Front
Work as for Back to * then cont as follows:
Change to 4mm needles and starting with a k row work 30(38) rows in St-st or until your work measures approx. 16.5(19)cm / 6½(7½)in from cast-on edge ending with a WS row.

Commence chart:
Row 1 (RS): With A, k53(61), join B and k1(1), with A, k4(4), with B, k1(1), with A, k4(4), with B, k1(1), with A, k to end.
Row 2 (WS): With A, p42(50), with B, p1(1), with A, p3(3), with B p1(1), with A, p3(3), with B, p1(1), with A, p to end.
Cont as set until row 71 of chart is complete.
Cont with A only and starting with a WS p row, work 21(27) rows in St-st, or until your work measures approx. 49(54)cm / 19(21½)in from cast-on edge, ending with a WS row.

Shape neck
Next row (RS): K43(50), turn your work so WS is facing, dec 1 st, p to end, turn. Cont on these sts, leaving remaining sts on hold.
** Dec 1 st at neck edge every row until 40(47) sts remain, then dec 1 st every other row until 35(42) sts remain.
Work 11(11) rows straight in St-st and cast off. ***
With RS facing, rejoin yarn at neck edge and k19(21), then slip these sts to holder for neckband and k to end of row.
Work as RH side from ** to ***.

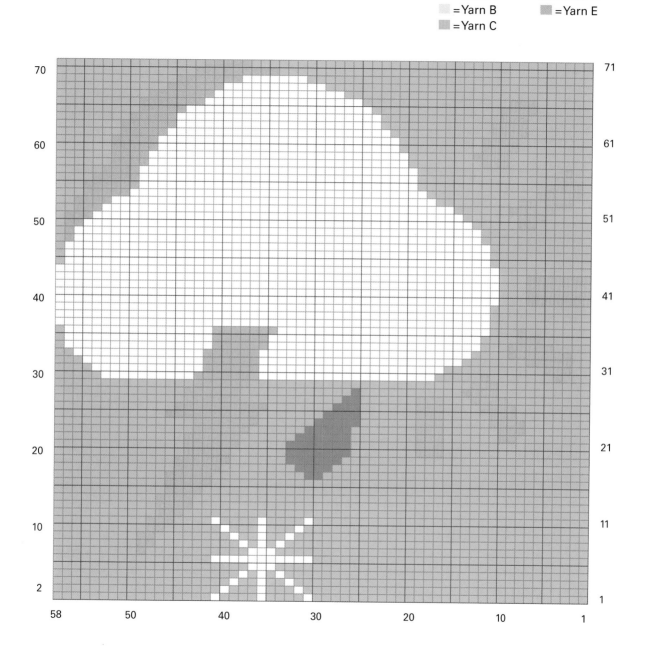

Sleeves (make two)

With 3.25mm needles and yarn A, cast on 48(52) sts.

Row 1 (RS): [K1, p1] rep to end. This row sets rib.

Work a further 14 rows in rib.

Next row (WS): Work as set in rib and **at the same time** inc 7(7) sts evenly across the row. 55(59) sts

Change to 4mm needles and starting with a k row, work in St-st and **at the same time** inc 1 st at each end of every sixth row a total of 11(13) times. 77(85) sts.

Cont straight in St-st until your work measures approx. 51(56)cm / 20(22)in from cast-on edge.

Cast off loosely.

Neckband

You can do this in one of two ways depending on your preference:

Using straight needles: Join Front and Back pieces at RH shoulder. Using a 3.25mm needle and A, beginning at LH shoulder with RS facing, pick up and k28(28) sts down LH front, work 19(21) held sts, pick up and k28(28) sts up RH side, work 35(37) held sts. 106(110) sts

Work in k1, p1 rib for 7 rows, knit 1 row, work rib for 7 rows. Cast off loosely in rib.

Using circular needles: Join both shoulder seams. With 3.25mm needle and A, beginning at LH shoulder with RS facing, pick up and k26(26) sts down LH front, work 19(21) held sts, pick up and k26(26) sts up RH side, work 35(37) held sts. 104(108) sts

Join for working in the round placing a marker to indicate beginning of round, work k1, p1 rib for 7 rounds, purl 1 round, work rib for 7 rounds. Cast off loosely in rib.

Making up

If using straight needles join LH shoulder.

Turn garment inside out so WS is facing, fold neckband over and loosely stitch into place on WS and so it does not pull tight.

Lay garment out flat, pin sleeves into position with centre point of cast-off edge lined up to shoulder seam and stitch into place.

Join side and sleeve seams.

Gently block to measurements shown on page 8.

Envy

Sellin ma flow i'm the star of the show

Envy

BEFORE YOU START

Materials
– Jarol Heritage DK – Yarn A: 5(6) balls in Bottle shade 117; Yarn B: 1 ball in Cream shade 100; Yarn C: 1 ball in Lime shade 137
– A pair of 3.25mm (US 3) knitting needles
– A pair of 4mm (US 6) knitting needles
– A set of 3.25mm (US 3) circular needles, 40cm (16in) long; (optional for working neckband in the round)
– Two stitch holders
– Tapestry needle

Sizes
S/M – To fit chest 86.5–91.5cm (34–36in), actual measurement 94cm (37in)
M/L – To fit chest 96.5–102cm (38–40in), actual measurement 108cm (42.5in)

Tension
22 sts and 28 rows to 10cm (4in) in stocking stitch on 4mm needles. Take time to check your tension and adjust as necessary to ensure an accurate fit.

SWEATER

Back
With 3.25mm needles and yarn A, cast on 98(110) sts.
Row 1 (RS): [K1, p1] rep to end.
This row sets rib.
Work a further 14(14) rows in rib.
Next row (WS): Work as set in rib and **at the same time** inc 7(11) sts evenly across the row. 105(121) sts *****
Change to 4mm needles and starting with a k row, work in St-st until your work measures approx. 58(63)cm / 23(25)in from cast-on edge ending with a WS row.

Shape shoulders
Next row (RS): Cast off 35(42) sts, k35(37), cast off 35(42) sts and place remaining sts on hold.

Front
Work as for Back to ***** then cont as follows:
Change to 4mm needles, yarn B and starting with a k row, work 36(40) rows in St-st or until your work measures approx. 18.5(20) cm / 7¼(8)in from cast-on edge ending with a WS row.

Commence chart:
Row 1 (RS): [With B, k3, with C, k1] rep 26(30) times to last st, with B, k1(1).
Row 2 (WS): With B, p1, [with B, p2, with C, p1, with B, p1] rep 26(30) times to end.
Cont as set until row 8 of chart is complete.
Cont with C only and work 36(40) rows in St-st or until your work measures approx. 34(37)cm / 13½(14½)in from cast-on edge ending with a WS row.

Commence chart again but working with Yarn C and A as follows:
Row 1 (RS): [With C, k3, with A, k1] rep 26(30) times to last st, with C, k1(1).

First chart
□ = Yarn C
■ = Yarn B

Second chart
□ = Yarn A
■ = Yarn C

Row 2 (WS): With C, p1, [with
C, p2, with A, p1, with C, p1] rep
26(30) times to end.
Cont as set until row 8 of chart is
complete.
Cont with A only and work 34(40)
rows in St-st, or until your work
measures approx. 49(54)cm /
19(21½)in from cast-on edge,
ending with a WS row.

Shape neck
Next row (RS): K43(50), turn your
work so WS is facing, dec 1 st, p
to end, turn. Cont on these sts,
leaving remaining sts on hold.
** Dec 1 st at neck edge every
row until 40(47) sts remain, then
dec 1 st every other row until
35(42) sts remain.
Work 11(11) rows straight in St-st
and cast off. ***
With RS facing, rejoin yarn at
neck edge and k19(21), then slip
these sts to holder for neckband
and k to end of row.
Work as RH side from ** to ***.

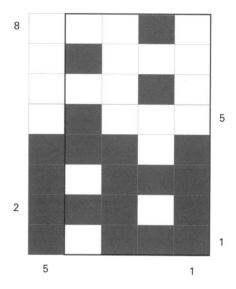

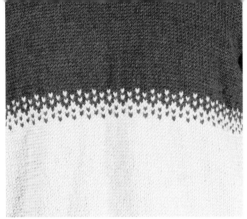

Sleeves (make two)

With 3.25mm needles and yarn A, cast on 48(52) sts.

Row 1 (RS): [K1, p1] rep to end. This row sets rib.

Work a further 14 rows in rib.

Next row (WS): Work as set in rib and **at the same time** inc 7(7) sts evenly across the row. 55(59) sts

Change to 4mm needles and starting with a k row, work in St-st and **at the same time** inc 1 st at each end of every sixth row a total of 11(13) times. 77(85) sts.

Cont straight in St-st until your work measures approx. 51(56)cm / 20(22)in from cast-on edge.

Cast off loosely.

Neckband

You can do this in one of two ways depending on your preference:

Using straight needles: Join Front and Back pieces at RH shoulder. Using a 3.25mm needle and A, beginning at LH shoulder with RS facing, pick up and k28(28) sts down LH front, work 19(21) held sts, pick up and k28(28) sts up RH side, work 35(37) held sts. 106(110) sts

Work in k1, p1 rib for 7 rows, knit 1 row, work rib for 7 rows. Cast off loosely in rib.

Using circular needles: Join both shoulder seams. With 3.25mm needle and A, beginning at LH shoulder with RS facing, pick up and k26(26) sts down LH front, work 19(21) held sts, pick up and k26(26) sts up RH side, work 35(37) held sts. 104(108) sts

Join for working in the round placing a marker to indicate beginning of round, work k1, p1 rib for 7 rounds, purl 1 round, work rib for 7 rounds. Cast off loosely in rib.

Making up

If using straight needles join LH shoulder. Turn garment inside out so WS is facing, fold neckband over and loosely stitch into place on WS and so it does not pull tight. Lay garment out flat, pin sleeves into position with centre point of cast-off edge lined up to shoulder seam and stitch into place.

Join side and sleeve seams. Gently block to measurements shown on page 8.

We once heard a rumour that a jumper might be too big a project for everyone. So what if you love our motif patterns but don't have the time or inclination to make a whole jumper?

Well, maybe you could make something smaller, like a cushion, or a hot water bottle cover or a scarf or a skirt. And you can. It's just MATHS.

HOW BIG DO YOU WANT YOUR PIECE OF KNITTING TO BE?

These equations are all based on a tension square of 22 stitches and 28 rows to 10cm (4in) square working in stocking stitch on 4mm needles.

	Width	**Length**
cm	Width of piece divided by (10 divided by 22) = number of stitches	Length of piece divided by (10 divided by 28) = number of rows

IF YOU WANT TO PLACE YOUR MOTIF IN A CENTRAL POSITION...

Count the number of stitches at the widest point of your motif, subtract from the total number of stitches and divide this number by 2 – this is how many stitches should be on either side of your chart.

Count the maximum number of rows in your motif, subtract this number from the total number of rows and divide this number by 2 – this is how many rows should be above and below your chart.

We can't calculate for every eventuality, but you get the picture. Literally.

OR JUST GO RENEGADE?

Polka dots

*Pattern repeats over
25 stitches and 30 rows*

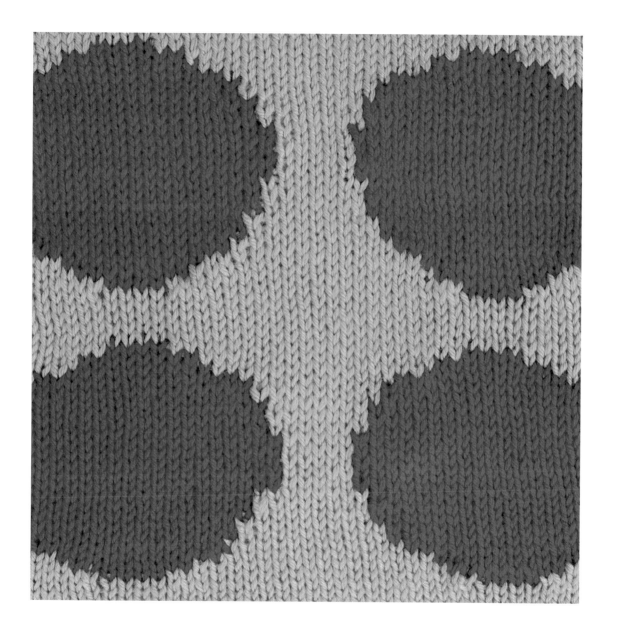

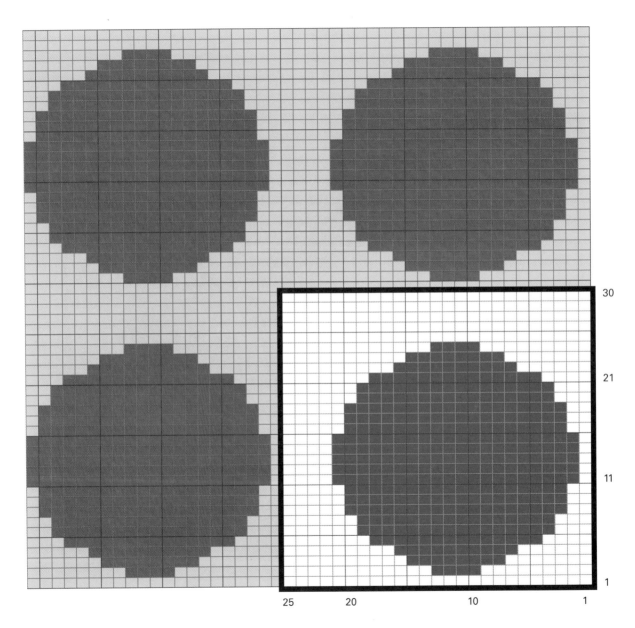

Stripes

*Pattern repeats over
infinite stitches and 12 rows*

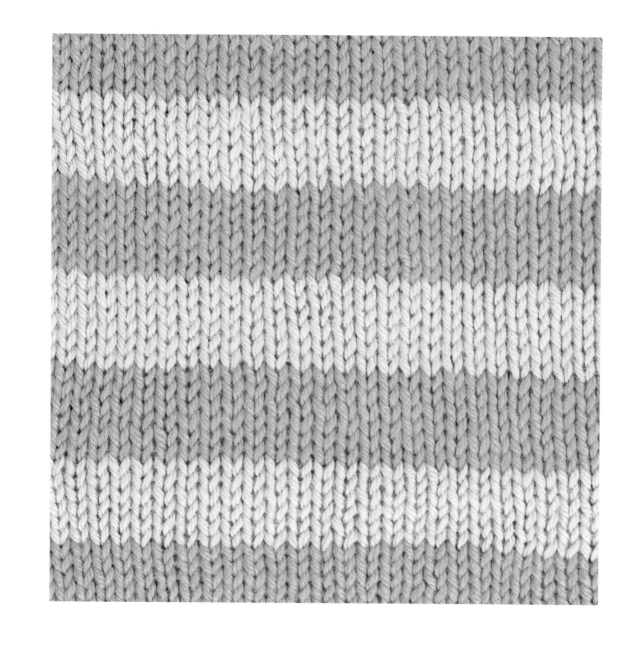

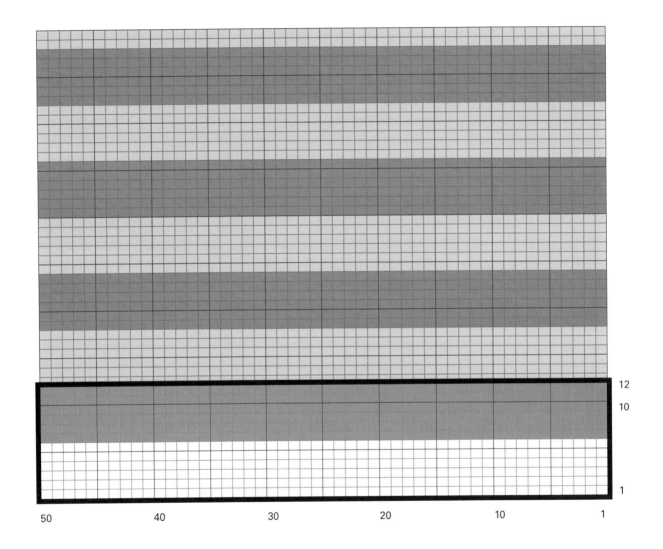

Zig zags

*Pattern repeats over
16 stitches and 10 rows*

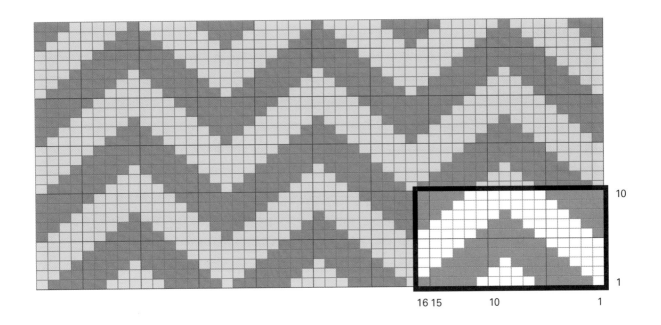

Diagonals

*Pattern repeats over
10 stitches and 20 rows*

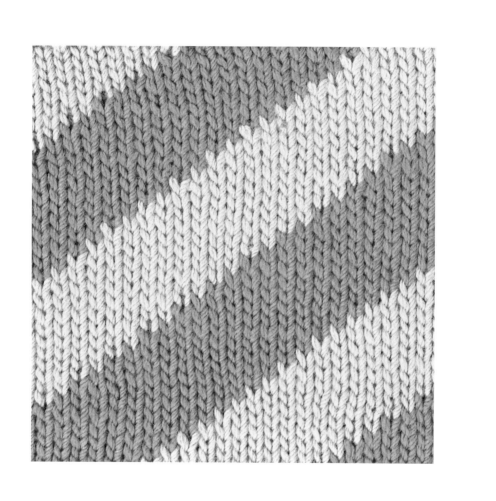

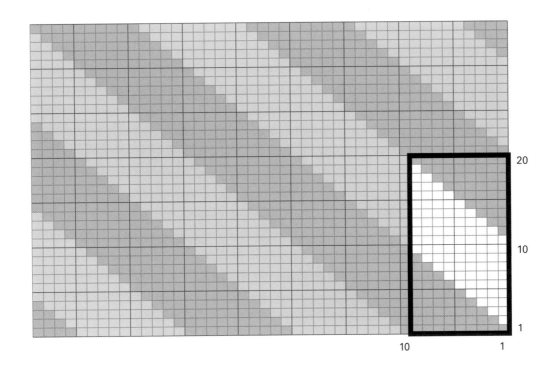

Checks

*Pattern repeats over
18 stitches and 20 rows*

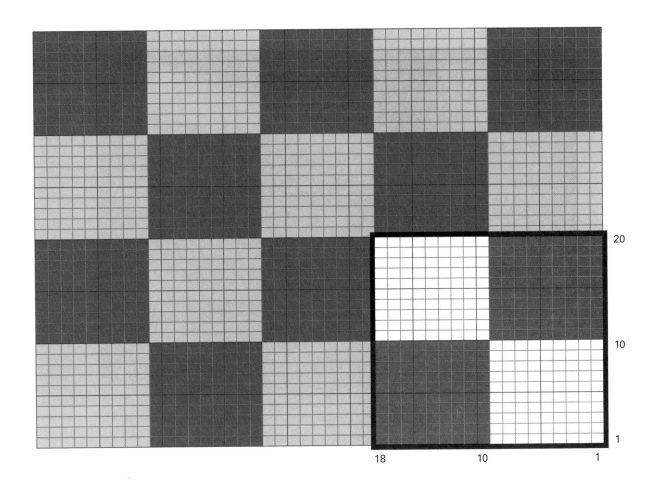

Hearts

Pattern repeats over
16 stitches and 19 rows

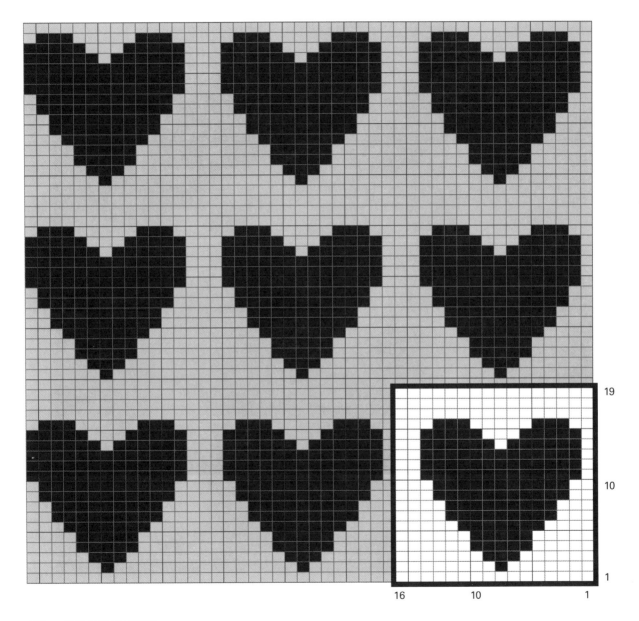

19

10

1

16   10   1

KNIT PARADE PLAYLIST

Are 'Friends' Electric?
Written by: Gary Numan, 1979
Performed by: Tubeway Army
5.24

Lucky Star
Written by: Madonna, 1983
Performed by: Madonna
5.37

Picture This
Written by: Jimmy Destri/
Debbie Harry/Chris Stein, 1978
Performed by: Blondie
2.56

Me Jane
Written by: PJ Harvey, 1993
Performed by: PJ Harvey
2.42

Mr Moustache
Written by: Kurt Cobain, 1989
Performed by: Nirvana
3.23

Paint It Black
Written by: Keith Richards/
Mick Jagger, 1966
Performed by: The Rolling Stones
3.45

Spring
Written by: Bob Stanley/
Pete Wiggs, 1991
Performed by: Saint Etienne
3.43

On Repeat
Written by: James Murphy, 2005
Performed by: LCD Soundsystem
8.01

Telephone
Written by: Beyoncé/LaShawn
Daniels/Lazonate Franklin/Lady
Gaga/Rodney Jerkins, 2009
Performed by: Beyoncé and
Lady Gaga
3.40

Bad Girls
Written by: Maya Arulpragasam/
Nate Hills/Marcella Araica, 2012
Performed by: M.I.A.
3.48

Weather Experience
Written by: Liam Howlett, 1992
Performed by: The Prodigy
8.06

Envy
Written by: Ms. Dynamite/
Megaman/The Twins/Asher D/
So Solid Crew, 2001
Performed by: So Solid Crew
5.49

WheresMeJumper
TheKnitParade
WheresMeJumper
WheresMeJumper

wheresmejumper.com

Founded by Beki Rymsza, Wheres Me Jumper launched online in 2010.

Working in collaboration with its customers to create custom-made, entirely unique pieces, the Manchester-based company is one of a kind.

If you've made one of the featured sweaters or designed your own piece of knitwear using this book as inspiration, send your photos to hello@wheresmejumper.co.uk – we'd love to see!

**This book wouldn't
have existed without:**

*Nick Beevors
My mum, Jacqueline
My nan, Winifred Violet*

And without some much-needed peer pressure from
Nick Beevors, Maria Da Silva Gordon, Porl Gordon
and Matt Tong there would be no Wheres Me Jumper!

THANKS A BILLION TO

Liz Newell – cool gal, designer and sanity saver

Beth Kojder – Wheres Me Jumper wonderwoman

Zoe Hancock – super stylist

Lou Adshead – the mother of make-up artists

Helen Kirkbright – kick-ass photographer

Paul Moffat – there ain't a problem that he can't fix

Sophie Parkes – this book is proof she knows her stuff

Music – for letting us run wild in the studio

**Our red-hot models,
in order of appearance:**

Sophie Bailey, Matt Maurer,
Sarah Morten, Ryan Lake,
Josie Hicklin, James West,
Max Howard, Danielle Jephson,
Rebecca Swarbrick, Josh Felton,
Bob Holland, Sarah Latimer,
Lisa Stannard, Mark Hudson,
Nic Chapman, Simon Edgar Lord,
Angela Smith (soon to be Maurer),
Nick Beevors, Yoshimi Miura,
David Peel, Elyse Blackshaw,
Conor Peden, Graham Hampton
and Rebecca Anderton

First published in the United Kingdom in 2013 by
Collins & Brown
10 Southcombe Street
London
W14 0RA

An imprint of Anova Books Company Ltd

Distributed in the United States and Canada by
Sterling Publishing Co, 387 Park Avenue South,
New York, NY 10016-8810, USA

ISBN 978-1-90844-937-5

A CIP catalogue record for this book is available from
the British Library.

10 9 8 7 6 5 4 3 2 1

Design by Elizabeth Newell
Photography by Helen Kirkbright

The publishers would like to thank Rachel Atkinson for her
work on checking the patterns, and Martin Norris for his swatch
photography.

Reproduction by Mission, Hong Kong
Printed by 1010 Printing International Ltd, China

Join our crafting community and find lots more books
to buy at LoveCrafts – we look forward to meeting you!